KISS

KEEP IT SHORT AND SIMPLE

And Make Writing Easy

Jacquie Ream

10/09

Book Publishers Network
P.O. Box 2256
Bothell • WA • 98041
PH•425-483-3040

Copyright © 2005 by Jacquie Ream

10 9 8 7 6 5 4 3 2

Printed in the United States of America

LCCN 2005920863
ISBN 1-887542-21-3

Editing: Julie Scandora
Cover Design: Lonny Stevens
Interior Layout: Stephanie Martindale

CONTENTS

INTRODUCTION

Your assignment is to write a paper. Begin at "Once...."

You're in the grip of the Beastly Assignment!! And there's no deliverance from that blank piece of paper. What to do? Tame that beast with a KISS!

Keep It Short and Simple. Any monster—short story, novel, poetry, essay, term paper, report, lecture notes, and even personal journals, letters and diaries—can be given a **KISS**. Using the **KISS** principle, no assignment is too difficult.

Where to begin? At the beginning. Read a book for information, and it will make that paper easier to write. The secret to understanding a short story, poem or novel is your emotional reactions: what made you laugh, cry; feel angry or sad? Gather facts and data for the term paper from reference materials in your own home and outside sources, and take short, concise notes.

Writing is easy. Really. It is a way for us to share our ideas and opinions with others.

Got a block on that short story, book report, term paper? Write about what you know: tell about a personal experience as it happened or fictionalize it; review the book ("see" it in your mind, calling up the memorable scenes) then outline the facts.

With a few short and simple rules of writing management, you'll be able to **KISS** that assignment good-bye.

Or maybe befriend a beast.

Chapter One

BE YOUR OWN
BEST FRIEND

The assignment looms large over little ole you, ready to eat you alive. Face it!

It's not as big as you might have thought. Break it into parts and the assignment is only a matter of putting your thoughts into words. It is as simple as A B C.

You had to learn the alphabet before you could read the words. Writing is a lot like learning your ABC's. You can learn simple skills that will make it easy to put your thoughts in order, to get from A to Z.

What makes it so hard to write down words and make sense out of an idea? Most often, it's because we think we can't do it right.

There are a few simple rules.

1st
Know your subject.

2nd
Trust yourself that you know what you know.

3rd
Organize, write and rewrite.

There are ways to make it easier, but you can't take all the work out of writing. You need to know the basics of writing before you can take shortcuts.

For instance, you won't always turn in an outline, but knowing how to do one, and do it well, will make it easier to organize and write your paper. To present that paper, you must know how to structure it: your ideas can be absolutely brilliant, but if the paper is a mess, you've lost your sparkle. If you're talking grades, looks count more than you can imagine.

And you can imagine. Once you've learned how to read a book, take notes and organize the material, then shaping your ideas into a paper is the least difficult part.

"No way!" you say? Writing is painful and hard and frustrating?

Ha! Writing is easy. Trust yourself. If you can read, you can write.

Taken step by step, an assignment is completed: gather the facts, organize the ideas in an outline, do a rough draft. Sentence by sentence, paragraph by paragraph, page by page, you finish the assignment.

The hardest part of writing the paper is the rewriting.

Not rewriting is the one shortcut that is often taken with regrettable consequences—misspelled words that are easily corrected; overlooked but important facts that are omitted; typos. If you look at rewriting as your ultimate line of defense, then the Beastly Assignment becomes a pet project.

And every pet needs a KISS.

Chapter Two

THE **KISS** PRINCIPLE

Keep It Short and Simple. Why?

It saves time. It saves the fingers from cramping. It saves the brain from overload. It saves your ideas from drowning in a sea of words.

To keep it short and simple, **you must know your subject.** To know your subject, answer five basic questions:

who
what
why
how
where.

Keep statements short and clear. Use your "voice"; put it in your own words. Reduce your idea to its simplest terms. Example:

A perfect short story:
The cat came back.

A perfect history project:
The cat was a kitten.

A perfect science project:
The cat can see in the dark.

A perfect social studies project:
The cat makes a good pet.

Writing a paper requires time, but fifteen or twenty minutes for each step will turn out a whole paper. It's really that simple.

Sometimes does it feel as if all your brains cells have dried up? The muscles in your hand have frozen stiff? Anxiety Attack! There is an antidote: PREPARATION.

Before you begin any project, be sure you understand what it is about. Ask questions of your teachers, librarians, parents, anyone who might help you understand the assignment. Give yourself plenty of time to do the assignment. Time can be your friend, not your enemy. If you have two weeks to turn in a book report, take ten minutes or so between other activities to read a chapter of the book, jot down notes or start outlining ideas during the first week. Don't do this on the same day as you are going to write the report. Do your fact finding, outline and rough draft *at least the day before* you write the final paper. Then give that final paper two days to "cool off" so that you can do last minute corrections.

Now that the Beastly Assignment is on a leash, let's walk through the steps of writing a paper from the beginning.

Chapter Three

THE BIRTH OF A PAPER

First, UNDERSTAND the assignment. Have a clear idea what your teacher expects from you. What kind of writing project is it? Is it a book report, essay, short story or term paper? Will you need a bibliography and/or title page? Do you need to put the final paper into a report cover, or can it be stapled (one staple in the left-hand corner) with a title page? Is the paper to be typed, can it be handwritten, how many pages minimum, and what is the format?

It is most common to use a computer word processing program that will facilitate the formatting of your paper. There are some differences in a typed or handwritten format and acceptable computer-generated formatting in word processors. One of the main differences in formats is <u>underlining</u>: for typed or handwritten papers, the title and chapters of novels, plays, magazine articles, newspapers, essays or journals must be <u>underlined</u>; if your word processor has the capability, *italicize* instead of underline. Quotation marks are used for titles of shorter works, such as articles from newspapers, journals, magazines, chapters of books and essays. If your teacher does not give a specific format for the paper, use these guidelines:

1. All papers, hand-written or typed, should be double-spaced (except for footnotes, endnotes, bibliography and long quotes).

2. If you cannot type your paper, use blue or black ink pen, and ruled notebook paper. Write on only one side of the paper.

3. To figure how many pages: one typed, double-spaced page is about 250 words.

4. Do not use onionskin or erasable bond typing paper. Use laser or inkjet printer paper.

5. Use a title page.

6. Top, bottom and right hand margins are 1"; left-hand margin is 1.5".

7. Rewrite and proofread carefully.

GATHER as much information as you can.

1. Libraries (school, county, city, branch, university) (See *Useful Information: LIBRARIES and LETTERS* on page 7)

2. The library quick reference telephone number

3. References: encyclopedias, the dictionary, atlas, almanac, educational television, magazines, newspapers, videos, computer with access to websites on the Internet

4. Chamber of Commerce, local businesses

5. Museums, organizations

6. Government agencies

7. Parents and other knowledgeable people.

Useful Information:
LIBRARIES and LETTERS

LIBRARIES are your resource center. Check out your local and school library, and get to know your librarians. Get to know the card catalog system to simplify your hunt for information; most, if not all, schools will be on computers that use a database as a card catalog. You will need to know how to access the computer and reference the material. Nationwide, all libraries are on-line and you must know a few basics to access information.

First, get a library card so that you can use all the resources at your library including on-line services, and check out books. You can access your local libraries from an Internet source, which means that you can do everything at home on your computer with Internet capability, or you can go to the library and use a computer there. The computer has a database that is the *card catalog* that will give you all the information for your research. As well as accessing books, you will be able to research encyclopedias, ebooks, journals, magazines, movies, music, periodicals, television and radio scripts, videos, and maps electronically. If you cannot find a book that you wish to check out and take home, you can request an inter-library loan and the book will be shipped to your local library. The books, magazines and newspapers in the library database are the same as the printed versions.

Second, you will need to find the name of your local library's website (example: King County Libraries is KCLS.org). The home page will have a format that simplifies searches for you. You will be able to search by

Keyword

Author/Name

Title

Subject

Publisher

Call Number (i.e., the Dewey Classification
Number that tells the location of the book)

Author/Title

Format

Languages

In Chapter Six under *Databases,* you will find
websites and **weblinks**. The chapter will detail electronic
submissions and how to document the resources found
on websites.

Should you find yourself in a library that is not on a
computerized database and that does not have a computer, there will be a CARD CATALOG. This is a system
of paper cards with a listing from A to Z of every book in
the library. There are four ways to look up a book:

1. Title card

2. Subject card (general)

3. Subject card (specific)

4. Author

You will find on these cards:

1. The call number (Dewey Classification Number) tells you where book is located

2. The author

3. A brief description of the book

4. Publisher and date of publication

5. A list of other categories where the book can
be found

For magazine and journal articles, use the *READ-
ERS' GUIDE TO PERIODICAL LITERATURE.* These are
volumes that index articles published in over one hun-
dred magazines and are found in the reference section
of the library.

In order to retrieve the article from the librarian at the periodical loan desk, you will need to write down:

1. Author's name
2. Article's title
3. What magazine
4. Date of the magazine
5. Page(s) of the article

The card catalog system is being replaced by computer. Do not be afraid of the computerized system. If you do not know how to use the computer to access the databases, ASK! The librarians are there to **help** you find information and use their systems. ASK, ASK ASK!

LETTERS written to local businesses, a Chamber of Commerce, museums, organizations, government agencies requesting information are an excellent resource for a term paper. Your letter should be:

1. Typed, if you can, or neatly written in black or blue ink.
2. Specific about what it is you want to know.
3. Brief.
4. In a business envelope affixed with proper postage, and with a self-addressed, stamped return envelope (SASE).
5. Mailed way ahead of your assignment due date.

Example of a Block Style Form Letter

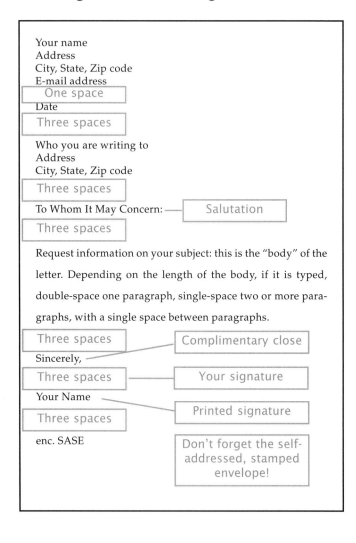

Your name
Address
City, State, Zip code
E-mail address
| One space |

Date
| Three spaces |

Who you are writing to
Address
City, State, Zip code
| Three spaces |

To Whom It May Concern: —— | Salutation |
| Three spaces |

Request information on your subject: this is the "body" of the letter. Depending on the length of the body, if it is typed, double-space one paragraph, single-space two or more paragraphs, with a single space between paragraphs.

| Three spaces | | Complimentary close |
Sincerely,

| Three spaces | —— | Your signature |
Your Name

| Three spaces | | Printed signature |

enc. SASE | Don't forget the self-addressed, stamped envelope! |

Take NOTES

Before that paper is written, you will have to make notes of some kind during your research. Once again, use the **KISS** principle to answer the questions you will find in the outline on pages 23-24, *EXAMPLE OF A SENTENCE OUTLINE: HOW TO READ A BOOK*. If you are reading your own copy of the text, use a highlighter and sticky notes. It is very rude to dog-ear a text book so use sticky notes. Sticky notes are simple and handy ways to mark text without defacing the book and especially useful if you are using reference texts that are not your own. Or use blank note cards or lined notebook paper. Note cards are easier to use because you can lay them out and play with the order when you do an outline. Notebook paper is handy, but use only one side.

The key to note taking is **focus**. Read with your topic in mind. Pay attention to the first sentence of a paragraph when you scan for facts. This will make it easier to find the facts you need without spending a lot of time reading all the article(s) or book.

1. Check the INDEX and TABLE OF CONTENTS pages of reference books to be sure your topic is covered in that book.

2. Read with questions to answer.

3. **KISS** notes: put into your own words what you read.

4. On your note cards or notebook paper, make headings with questions that focus on the topic of your paper.

5. When you find a fact you will use, **write down the page number** and what source(s) it comes

from: you will need this for the bibliography and referencing a quote.

6. Check for accuracy of facts and exact words in quotes.

7. List the sources of information:
   BE SURE TO NOTE:
   ♦ the author
   ♦ title of the reference book (include the volume number)
   ♦ where it was published
   ♦ the publisher and year.

8. Take a break.

ORGANIZE Your Data

Think of an outline as the skeleton of the paper, the research as the bones of the skeleton, and the "fleshed out" writing as the body of the paper.

1. Start with a title for your paper, making it very clear what it is you are writing about: "Assignment #101," or get creative and make a play on words or use a quote from what you have read that "says it perfectly." For the short story, novel or poem, the title is as important as the

body of the work. But for any paper, *the title is an arrow* to let the reader know what the paper is about.

2. Outlines are handy to make sense out of notes by grouping ideas, then adding and subtracting facts. Or use an outline before you research, making the five basic questions (who, what, where, why and how) the major topics, then fill in the answers from your research. After you've arranged your notes by topics or sentences, then look for and plug up any gaps with facts and figures.

M & M s
The Mechanics and Magic of Writing

Knowing the simple mechanics of writing eases anxiety and allows the magic to happen. Put the "editor," that beastie with the nagging whisper that demands perfection, in another room until needed for rewriting your paper. Use the critical voice first for gathering the information and organizing and last for rewriting a final draft.

In the middle of the writing process is chaos. Allow chaos to work for you, releasing creative energy. Let those ideas hatch all at once, then group them into clusters as shown on the following page. This illustration is an example of the first round of ideas. Use memories and all five senses (hearing, smell, taste, sight and touch) to connect with the ideas you are writing on paper. Play with the words and find new ways to express your ideas.

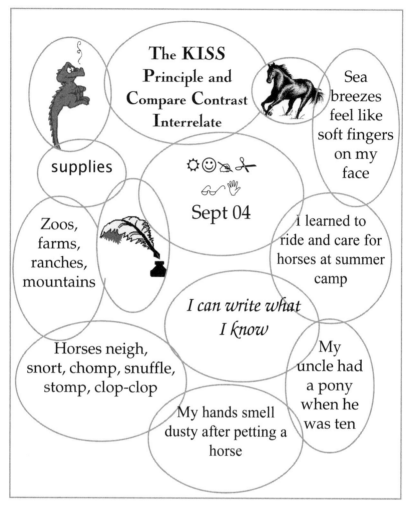

The **KISS** **P**rinciple and **C**ompare **C**ontrast **I**nterrelate

Sea breezes feel like soft fingers on my face

supplies

Sept 04

Zoos, farms, ranches, mountains

I learned to ride and care for horses at summer camp

I can write what I know

Horses neigh, snort, chomp, snuffle, stomp, clop-clop

My uncle had a pony when he was ten

My hands smell dusty after petting a horse

You will find that as you do layers of thoughts like this (no matter how messy it gets!) magically, the theme of your paper will emerge. Write! Write! Write! Set the paper aside and come back tomorrow. Now give your pet a treat and call out the editor.

Chapter Four

WRITE THE PAPER

One of the most useful and important tools for writing essays and reports is the *COMPARE, CONTRAST, and INTERRELATE (CCI)* formula. Once you understand the components, you can organize your thoughts quickly and within a structure, making it easy to do long reports or short, timed essays. Memorize these definitions!

Compare: (think similar characteristics) tell how two (or more) subjects are alike. Example: cars and motorcycles are means of transportation and are faster than walking; both have engines using fuel; both require licensing to ensure a certain degree of driver competency.

Contrast: (think opposite characteristics) tell how two subjects are different. Example: cars have four wheels, motorcycles have two; cars use more fuel than motorcycles; a motorcyclist is exposed to the weather, other cars, and road hazards more so than a driver of a car.

Interrelate: (think how the similar and opposite characteristics make a whole) using the subjects, show the relationship between them, using comparisons and contrasts from previous paragraphs. Example: While it is cheaper to own and operate a motorcycle, a car is much safer. Overall, motor-operated accidents are far greater than other modes of transportation, but the driver is safer in a car than on a motorcycle.

Let's apply this to a timed essay test, such as the SAT. The hypothetical question on the test is to write a short essay defining the term *classic* in literature.

First, take a deep breath and exhale slowly. You have just done a book report on Anna Sewell's book, *Black Beauty*. You have read Walter Farley's *Black Stallion* and Marguerite Henry's *Misty of Chincoteague*. Hmm...these are considered classics of children's literature...all about horses, with different themes.

Okay, take another breath, exhale and think how to narrow the subject matter down to a specific topic. "Classic" as in old, but well-maintained cars from the past, still being driven, still able to get from one place to another and looking very good. "Classic" as in music, a different listening experience than rock & roll, grunge or jazz. "Classic" as in fashion, clothing, hair and beauty. "Classic" as in timeless, Greek, Roman, Hellenic ages.

Take another breath, exhale. What would these three books have in common that make each one a literary classic? Well, who, young or old, doesn't love a good horse story? Adventure! A special understanding with a wild, beautiful creature that could happen to me, too! I can see myself riding Black Beauty, the Black or Misty. I could be a hero; I could love that horse and save him/her, too. I would treat a horse with respect and do all the right things for a horse. I would work hard, too, and earn money to keep a horse....I could imagine myself in that story. In other words, the book is as meaningful today as at the time it was written.

Compare: three stories about horses...full of factual and historical information, educational...appealing to a sense of adventure in the reader...tapping into the emotions, such as anger, joy, anxiety and wonder...making sense...giving the reader a larger picture of the time, place and events...longing and resolution. Rewarding... for the reader, for the fictional characters that seem real enough to have actually lived.

Contrast: *Black Beauty* is more moralistic, can appeal to older and younger readers, both girls and boys; *The Black Stallion* is adventurous and, because the hero is a boy, might appeal especially to male readers; *Misty of Chincoteague* seems written for a very young audience, with emphasis on family.

Interrelate: no matter that most readers will never own a horse or pony, the desire to do so will always spark the imagination of girls and boys. All three stories tell of a love for animals, the relationship of girl/boy to horse and how the animal is treated or mistreated, which is a relevant issue of all ages. Courage is a shared attribute of human and animal; responsibility to care for one another is also highlighted in the relationship of people to animal. These are core values that never are dated.

Let's suppose that it takes you three minutes to mentally arrange the components. You have 27 minutes left to write an essay. You know this: KISS! *Keep It Short and Simple.*

ALL writing projects have the same basic structure

A BEGINNING,

A MIDDLE,

AND AN END.

What could be simpler? The key is to know your subject, then write about what you know.

The beginning will be your opening paragraph, making a statement about the topic, which is to define the term, *classic*. You have chosen to narrow that down to children's literature, using as examples, *Black Beauty*, *The Black Stallion*, and *Misty of Chincoteague*.

Opening paragraph: You have thought this through: classic cars, music, fashion, literature...what is common to all? There is something that relates to all ages, of all times.

Use what you know

You have set it up to use the compare, contrast, interrelate formula

Compare

Emotional reactions refer to introduction statement. What made you feel angry or sad, etc.

You are going to use examples that define classic

A book written in another era that captures the imagination of a modern reader and has meaning today is a literary classic. In children's literature, three books are considered classic. They are *Black Beauty*, by Anna Sewell, *The Black Stallion*, by Walter Farley, and *Misty of Chincoteague*, by Marguerite Henry. Although different in many ways, each book illustrates a timelessness that appeals to young and old readers even today.

Throughout the horse adventures are lessons that are relevant to any age. Reading about Black Beauty can stir the **emotions**, making a person want to speak out courageously about the mistreatment of animals. Paul and Maureen (*Misty*) work hard to buy two ponies, Phantom and her foal, Misty, and share like **reactions** about mistreatment of farm animals and wild ponies. Alec frequently expresses his **concern** for the safety and health of his stallion, the Black. **Kindness, giving one's time and attention, loving unconditionally, accepting responsibility, and working hard** are lessons that are just as important today as in the 1800's and early 1900's.

Emotional reactions refer to introduction statement. What made you feel angry or sad, etc.

Contrast

Black Beauty is more moralistic than either *The Black Stallion* or *Misty*, with its crusade against alcoholism and mistreatment of animals. *The Black Stallion* is a boy's adventure, whereas *Misty* is about a brother's and sister's shared goal to purchase two wild ponies. But in each instance, the reader **wants to be there in that time and be a part of** the adventures, misfortunes and companionship of the people and animals.

Another element of your definition of classic

All three stories draw the reader into the mind and heart of the characters; *Black Beauty* is more immediate because of first person point of view. The reader wants the best for Black Beauty, for Alec and the Black Stallion, and for Paul, Maureen and Phantom with her colt, Misty. There is a satisfying ending to each story, after hardships and dramatic events that threaten the horses. Very young readers will appreciate *Misty of Chincoteague*, the story centered on one conflict and resolution, within a family structure; i.e., Paul and Maureen earning the money to purchase mother and foal. *The Black Stallion* is a thrilling adventure for boys and girls who can follow the continuing saga in a

Interrelate

series about The Black. *Black Beauty* is a more in-depth look into the society and the whys and wherefores of the times that Black Beauty lived, with multiple conflicts and not-so-happy endings all the time.

Although technology has replaced the working horse, who doesn't love a good story about a horse? Anyone who has ever professed a love of horses should read *Misty of Chincoteague*, *The Black Stallion*, and *Black Beauty*, three of the best classic children's books. The reader can experience and learn from the determination of Paul and Maureen to earn enough money to purchase the ponies, Alec's own maturity in his adventures with the Black Stallion and Black Beauty's chronicles of a life of hardship and survival, the good and bad in people and ultimately having faith rewarded. The reader cheers, despairs and triumphs with each character's trial and resolution, and gains an appreciation for basic values shown through the experiences that each one goes through during the course of the story. Each book is a good example of a children's classic, for they all relate to readers of yesterday, today and tomorrow.

Conclusion

You can make bold statements after presenting your arguments

Restate what the original question of the essay—theme—is

If you have time left, and you should have a minute, scan for bloopers, making your corrections as neatly as possible. Before the SATs, practice writing short, timed essays and you will have the confidence to write under pressure using **KISS** and the **CCI formula**.

REWRITE

1. If possible, set the completed first draft aside for a day or two.

2. Good writing is revision (re:again/vision:to see)
    *   Is there any way to make the idea clearer?
    *   Does that sentence make sense?
    *   Is too much said or too little?

3. And **always, always** check for spelling and punctuation. Make a friend and be a friend: get someone else to proofread for you if you can. Go over that paper carefully for errors, for little mistakes can be deadly.

Arranging the Bones:
THE OUTLINE

EXAMPLE OF A TOPIC OUTLINE: This is the outline I used to write this book.
I. Starting with an Idea
    A. The **KISS** principle
        1. *Keep It Short and Simple*
        2. Applying **KISS** to the assignment
    B. How to Read a Book
        1. For content
            a. Title
            b. Main character
            c. Most important event that happens to main character
            d. Conflict/resolution/change in main character
        2. For Reference
            a. Index

b. Table of contents
C. Research
    1. How to take notes
    2. What to do with them
    3. Resources: what and how to use them
D. Outline
    1. Types
      a. Topic
      b. Sentence
    2. Format
II. Paper
  A. What Kind
     1. Short story
     2. Term
     3. Essay
     4. Report
     5. Letter
     6. Journal
  B. Elements of Writing
     1. Beginning, middle and end
     2. Glossary of definitions
     3. Active verbs/active ideas
     4. Rewriting/revision (to see again)
  C. Presentation
     1. Covers
     2. Paragraphs
     3. Margins
     4. Headings
     5. Footnotes
     6. Endnotes
     7. Bibliography
     8. References
  D. Problem Areas
     1. Grammar
     2. Punctuation
     3. Proofreading (editing)

4. Parts of speech
5. Incomplete sentences
6. Spelling

EXAMPLE OF A SENTENCE OUTLINE: The assignment might be to write a paper on *How to Read a Book*.

I. There are ways to read a book.
  A. **Pay attention to details.**
    1. Note the title: it is an arrow, a direction for the story.
    2. <u>Underline</u> or note in some way the main character.
    3. <u>Underline</u> or note in some way the most important event.
    4. When or why does the main character change?
II. Make sense out of the book.
  A. What sense does the title make?
    1. What did the title tell me?
    2. Where in the story did it make sense?
    3. Why that title?
  B. Who is the main character?
    1. What is the name of the main character?
      a. Does the name have another meaning; i.e., is it a reference to a familiar, known person, place or thing?
      b. If it isn't obvious who the main character is, the story is written in the first person, and you may assume the author is the main character.
    2. What are the age, gender and vital statistics of the main character?
    3. Is the main character a good guy or bad?
    4. How does the main character act, smart or dumb? (What is the character's motivation?)

C. What is the most important event that happens
    to the main character?
    1. Why and how does it matter to the main
       character?
    2. Does the main character change because of it?
D. How did you, the reader, feel?
    1. Did you like the story?
    2. Why or why not?
      a. Did you believe the author?
      b. Could the change(s) really have happened
        and made a difference to the main
        character?
    3. Did you like the main character?
    4. Have you ever had a similar experience?
    5. Did the story make a difference to you? Did
      you think, act or feel differently because you
      read the story?
    6. Would you read the story again and enjoy it?

The *most important event* is also defined as *conflict*.
There are three basic types of conflict in which a literary
character is engaged in the story:

      a. main character against himself
      b. main character against another
        (protagonist/antagonist)
      c. main character against God (or Nature)

The *change* is also defined as *resolution*: how the conflict is resolved (**re-solved**), or settled.

OUTLINE FOR A BOOK REPORT: BLACK BEAUTY

I. Title: *BLACK BEAUTY, The Autobiography of a Horse,* by Anna Sewell
   A. Most important character: horse, Black Beauty
   B. Autobiography: the horse narrates his story
II. The main character
   A. Black Beauty
   B. His story from birth to old age
   C. Told first person, from Black Beauty's point of view
   D. Wise and insightful telling of his life's events
   E. His story illustrates morals
      1. Cruelty and ignorance that make people act badly
      2. Kindness and humanness are man's good qualities
      3. Alcohol makes people act badly toward animals and other people
III. Examples of good and bad events
   A. Fashion
      1. Bobbing horses' tails
      2. Checkreins
      3. Dangerous sporting events
   B. Alcohol
      1. People act cruelly and irrationally because of alcohol
         a. Rueben Smith
   C. Horses ill-treated
      1. Flogged
      2. Underfed
      3. Improperly exercised
      4. Overworked
   D. Kindness toward animals
      1. Clean stables
      2. Enough food, water and exercise
      3. Kind words

IV. Importance of *Black Beauty*
- A. Historical look at England in 1800's
- B. Treatment of animals
- C. Some customs and morals of the time
- D. Significance to modern readers
    1. Kindness toward animals
    2. Kindness toward people
    3. Bad to act out of ignorance

An Example of a
WRITING ASSIGNMENT

Title Page Format

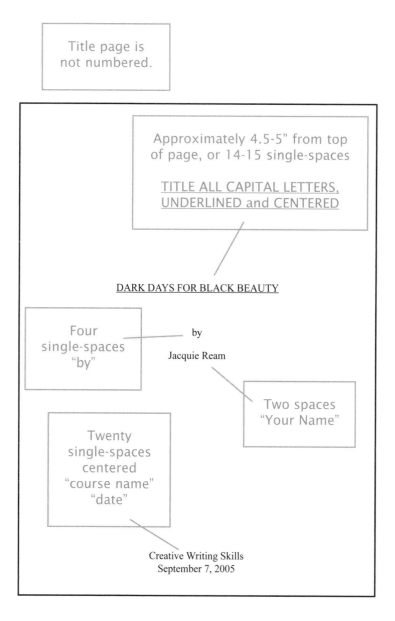

Title page is not numbered.

Approximately 4.5-5" from top of page, or 14-15 single-spaces

TITLE ALL CAPITAL LETTERS, UNDERLINED and CENTERED

DARK DAYS FOR BLACK BEAUTY

Four single-spaces "by"

by

Jacquie Ream

Two spaces "Your Name"

Twenty single-spaces centered "course name" "date"

Creative Writing Skills
September 7, 2005

First Page Format

Title is 3" from the top of the page

TITLE IS CENTERED AND UNDERLINED,
ALL CAPITALS

Indent five spaces

DARK DAYS FOR BLACK BEAUTY

Three spaces

There, on the desk, blank sheets of paper lay beside the children's novel, Black Beauty, The Autobiography of a Horse. The author, Anna Sewell, wrote only this one book, her attempt to educate and reform the public's accepted abuse of animals and the evils of alcohol. Published in 1877, Black Beauty quickly became assigned reading by school teachers and librarians. Today, the novel is considered a "classic," still required reading and educational for students of all ages, and a good example to use for a book report.

Topic sentence

1.5" left-hand margin

Right-hand margin 1"

Black Beauty, a thoroughbred horse, was born on an estate in England, in the late 1800's. Even though it is a long time ago, in the horse and buggy days of England, the speech and customs are interesting to a reader, and the morals still apply today. The story is the autobiography of Black Beauty, told from his point of view about his life (first person narrative). It is about the good and bad treatment of horses by people, and the suffering of inno-cent animals.

Lead sentence   Follow with examples

The bad things that happen to Black Beauty and the other horses are caused by people's ignorance and bad effects of drinking

Text is double-spaced   Bottom margin is 1"

No name or page number on first page

Top margin 1"   Header 1/2"   Ream 2

alcohol. For instance, it is cruel to bob horses' tails and to strap their heads unbearably high for fashion, or to have to shoot a horse for a broken leg because of a hunting accident. Rueben Smith, a good man "but too madly drunk to notice anything"[1] fell and died riding Black Beauty too fast going to a tavern; because of a loose horseshoe that Rueben Smith would not have fixed, Black Beauty's knees were torn and blemished. As a result, the earl sold Black Beauty to a livery stable. From then on, Black Beauty went through many more bad experiences, mostly because people did not treat horses humanely. Horses were beaten, underfed, exercised improperly, or worked like machines, overloaded until they died from exhaustion.

There were some good people in the story that knew how to take care of horses. Squire Gordon, who owned Black Beauty's mother, too, "was a good, kind man. He gave us food, good lodging and kind words"[2]. John Manly was kind and knew how to handle horses. James, a stableboy at the Gordons' estate, rescued Black Beauty from a stable fire. Joe Green tried to stop a man from flogging his horses, making it his business to interfere with cruelty and oppression. Jeremiah Barker, a cab driver, and his family really loved Black Beauty, renaming him Jack, and gave him decent working and living conditions. And at the last, Mr.

> Make sure to balance your statements with facts, quotes from the research material

[1] Anna Sewell, Black Beauty (New York: Children's Classic, 1954) p. 113
[2] Ibid., p. 10

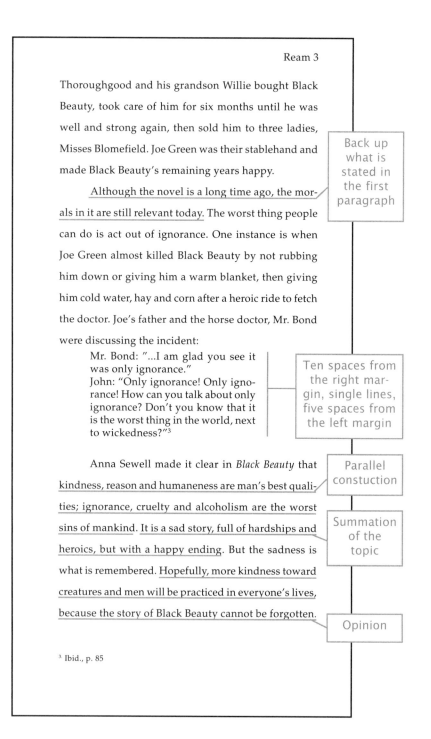

Ream 3

Thoroughgood and his grandson Willie bought Black Beauty, took care of him for six months until he was well and strong again, then sold him to three ladies, Misses Blomefield. Joe Green was their stablehand and made Black Beauty's remaining years happy.

Back up what is stated in the first paragraph

Although the novel is a long time ago, the morals in it are still relevant today. The worst thing people can do is act out of ignorance. One instance is when Joe Green almost killed Black Beauty by not rubbing him down or giving him a warm blanket, then giving him cold water, hay and corn after a heroic ride to fetch the doctor. Joe's father and the horse doctor, Mr. Bond were discussing the incident:

> Mr. Bond: "...I am glad you see it was only ignorance."
> John: "Only ignorance! Only ignorance! How can you talk about only ignorance? Don't you know that it is the worst thing in the world, next to wickedness?"[3]

Ten spaces from the right margin, single lines, five spaces from the left margin

Anna Sewell made it clear in *Black Beauty* that kindness, reason and humaneness are man's best qualities; ignorance, cruelty and alcoholism are the worst sins of mankind. It is a sad story, full of hardships and heroics, but with a happy ending. But the sadness is what is remembered. Hopefully, more kindness toward creatures and men will be practiced in everyone's lives, because the story of Black Beauty cannot be forgotten.

Parallel constuction

Summation of the topic

Opinion

[3] Ibid., p. 85

Format for
FOOTNOTES and ENDNOTES

In the preceding book report, "Dark Days for Black Beauty," there are three examples of footnotes. All the information for the footnote can be found in the front title page and the copyright page of the reference book.

For magazine quotes, the footnotes list:
1. Name of the author
2. Title of the article
3. Name of the magazine, *italicized* or <u>underlined</u>
4. Date the article appeared
5. Page number of the article

Example of a magazine footnote:

[1] Caplan, Robert D. "Black Beauty Returns." *Time Magazine* 19 March 2004: p. 113.

For encyclopedias, footnotes list:
1. Title of the entry
2. Name of encyclopedia, *italicized* or <u>underlined</u>
3. Edition number
4. Year published
5. Page of the entry

Example of an encyclopedia footnote:

[1] "Black Beauty Returns." *Encylcopedia Britannica* 15th ed. 1987: p. 113.

The same information that is needed in the footnotes and endnotes is included in the bibliography. All quotes are numbered. Make sure all the page numbers agree with the designated quote!

[1] Anna Sewell *Black Beauty* (New York: Children's Classic, 1954) p. 113
[2] Ibid., p. 10

³ Ibid., p. 85

Most word processors on the computer automatically provide space for the footnote. If you are typing your report, allow at least one inch at the bottom of the page (above the one-inch margin for a footnote).

It is difficult to judge how much space you will need for more than one footnote. If it is the same book all the way through the report, use the Latin word "Ibid.," meaning "in the same place" or "opt. cit.," meaning "in the work previously quoted" for a previously quoted reference.

If instead of footnotes you are going to use endnotes, you will still number the quotes starting with ¹, but put the references at the end of the document. As an example, let's use the end of "Dark Days for Black Beauty" with endnotes instead of footnotes.

Anna Sewell made it clear in *Black Beauty* that kindness, reason and humaneness are man's best qualities; ignorance, cruelty and alcoholism are the worst sins of mankind. It is a sad story, full of hardships and heroics, but with a happy ending. But the sadness is what is remembered. Hopefully, more kindness toward creatures and men will be practiced in everyone's lives, because the story of Black Beauty cannot be forgotten.

| Two spaces |

Endnotes

| Two spaces |

¹ Anna Sewell, Black Beauty (New York: Children's Classic, 1954) p. 113
² Ibid., p. 10
³ Ibid., p. 85

Example of a BIBLIOGRAPHY

This is the order:
1. Last name of the author
2. Comma
3. First name of the author
4. Period
5. Two spaces
6. The title of the book, *italicized* or <u>underlined</u>
7. Period
8. City of publication
9. Colon
10. Name of publisher
11. Comma
12. Date of publication
13. Period

Inside the reference book, on the backside of the title page, you will find the city where the book was published, the publisher, and the year the book was published.

Here is an example of a bibliography of the references I used for this book.

BIBLIOGRAPHY is centered on line 4, all capital letters and underlined.

BIBLIOGRAPHY

Two double spaces

First line is a hanging indent - 5 spaces

DeVries, Mary A. *The Practical Writer's Guide.* New York: New American Library/Signet, 1986.

Flesch, Ph.D., Rudolf and A.H. Lass. *A New Guide to Better Writing.* New York: Popular Library/Harper & Row, 1949.

Double space between each entry

James, Elizabeth and Carol Barkin. *How to Write a TERM PAPER.* New York: Lothrop, Lee & Shepard Books, 1980.

Kahn, Steve. *How to WRITE a Winning Term Paper.* Connecticut: Longmeadow Press, 1988.

McCormick, Mona. *The New York Times Guide to Reference Materials.* Chicago: Popular Library/Quadrangle Books, 1971.

Nurnberg, Maxwell and Morris Rosenblum. *How to Build a Better Vocabulary.* New York: Popular Library/Prentice-Hall, 1961.

Strunk, Wm. Jr. and E.B. White. *Elements of Style.* New York: Macmillan Publishing Co., Inc., 1979.

Turabain, Kate L. *STUDENT'S GUIDE for Writing College Papers, 3rd edition.* Chicago: University of Chicago Press, 1976.

Chapter Five

REVIEW: CATCHING THOSE BLOOPERS

BLOOPERS are those little things that undo a perfect paper. Like:

> Misspelled words
>
> Typos
>
> Run-on sentences
>
> Grammar
>
> Punctuation
>
> Tense agreement
>
> Format
>
> Onion-skin or erasable bond paper

Use this checklist to go over your paper before calling it quits. Misspelled words can be easily corrected; look up a word and be sure, or use the spell checker if your computer program has one.

Typos are hard to catch because we read what we think should be there. Ask someone to go over your paper and look for transposed letters. It is all right to pencil lightly a correction or two, but if there are more than three, redo.

Run-on sentences make it hard to figure out what idea is being presented and make the reader wonder if you know your subject and know that it is better to say one thing at a time rather than trying to cram a whole bunch of ideas into one long, long sentence. Confusing, to say the least.

Grammar, punctuation and tense agreement are important. Subject and verb must agree. If you start in the present tense, stay in the present (or past, past perfect, future) throughout the paper. The exception to this rule is when you are using a quote; then use the exact wording from the text. Put a period at the end of every sentence. If you are unsure where and when to use commas, semi-colons and colons, refer to a dictionary. Loads of useful information can be found in the front and back of a dictionary.

Be sure you know what your teacher expects of your final paper. The format, or how it looks, is very important to present your ideas dressed in the right style.

Use good bond paper. Onion-skin and erasable bond typing paper make it difficult to read; the ink smears and smudges on the paper and it is hard on the eyes to read. Present your paper, neatly—*a title page is a must*—and in a report cover. First impressions can make the grade!

Chapter Six

ELECTRONIC SUBMISSIONS OR E-SUB

Your pet has grown and needs another training session, or he will revert back to being a beastly assignment. Sooner, or no later than college, you will be asked to submit your paper electronically. The best resource is the Internet, which necessitates a computer that can access on-line sites of the Internet, or Web. If you are new to the Internet, affectionately known as a "newbie," familiarize yourself with Internet manners, or netiquette, so that you are not mistaken for a beastie. One of the best Websites is Judith Kallos' http://www.getnetiquette .com/courtesy4.html.

Once you have logged onto the Internet, you can type a general category (example: **writing styles**) into the search engine window and scroll through the list of Websites for the specific information you are researching. *Note: always type in lowercase letters.*

Research done on the Internet **must be documented**. Don't think for a moment that you can use information from Websites and not give credit. And while on the subject, do not ever, *ever* plagiarize. At the very least, you will be embarrassed; most likely, you will fail the course and you could be expelled.

There are many **well-known** Websites, also called paper mills, that sell term papers. There are also many competent programs that detect recycled term papers. You can be sure that the instructor is aware of the Websites and uses a recognition program.

Many professors have set up their own guidelines. Ask your instructor what format to use. If the instructor is not specific, then pick a standard format. Another excellent resource for documentation is Michael Harvey's *The Nuts and Bolts of College Writing*; his Website is http://www.nutsandboltsguide.com.

Using the Internet is a rapidly evolving process, but there are rules to format papers being sent via the Internet. There are three acceptable standard formats to use:

APA (American Psychology Association)

MLA (Modern Language Association)

Chicago (Chicago Manual of Style) or Turabain Style.

There are some differences in typed papers and electronically-submitted papers. For example, in submitted papers, there is one space after punctuation, and *italics* are used for titles. If the paper is handwritten or typed, then the title is underlined and two spaces are used after a period or colon. You must have, at the very least, in the footnote: Title of Document, URL (this is the Internet address, or Uniform Resource Locator), date you accessed the Website and Author (last name, first name).

The information presented here is from the most knowledgeable site for submitting electronically and the URL is: http://www.apastyle.org/elecmedia.html.[1] The following model is cited from the APA Style/Electronic media and URLs[2]:

http://www.apa.org/monitor/oct00/elecmedia.html

| Protocol (optional) | Host name | Path to document | File name of specific document (optional) |

Copy and paste the URL from the browser window into your document; double check if you are transcribing the URL to be sure it is correct. If the URL is long, **do not** put a hyphen to break a URL; break at the slash or before a period. Test the URL to be sure that it refers to the right site location. Keep in mind that the Websites change without any notice and a reference in your paper may not be valid after you have submitted your final copy. **It is very important to date the references; sites change constantly and the one you cite may not be there the next time.** You must document carefully and do so as you go along, in draft form. That way, you will have a record of what you have done.

For the final draft, after it has been spell-checked and visually re-read for errors, you must save it in a format to send electronically. The most common for college papers is *rtf* (rich text format) in *Microsoft Word*. To do this, click on "file," then "save as," then save as type: Rich Text Format (*.rtf). If you are submitting in another word processing program, make sure that you

[1] 5th edition of APA, Publication Manual©(2001), APAStyle.org, Electronic References, doc: Electronic Media http://www.apastyle. org/ elecmedia.html, August 4, 2004
[2] Ibid.

can submit properly in *rtf*. Much of the formatting of the paper will be done automatically by the word processing program if you familiarize yourself with the basics. ***Know your program; save yourself a headache!***

You must have a means to transmit the file to the instructor. This is done by attaching the file to an email that you will send to your instructor's email address. So, be sure to have the right email address for your instructor! Before submitting a paper for the first time, it would be wise to practice emailing attachments to a friend. Since you *have* allowed enough time for re-writing, ask your friend to review your paper for content and context.

Once your paper is proof-read and the corrections made, then it is ready to be submitted in person or e-mailed. You have mastered the writing skills you need to go onto the next assignment with confidence and assurance. *Keep It Short and Simple* and you can tame any Beast with a KISS!

GLOSSARY

Active voice: verbs that show the subject doing rather than being.

Allegory: a story, like a fable, that teaches and explains, in which the people, places and events have another meaning; in other words, the people, places and events are symbolic.

Allusion: indirect reference to a familiar idea, i.e., "an eye for an eye" refers to the Biblical quote: "...eye for eye, tooth for tooth, hand for hand, foot for foot." Deuteronomy 19:21.

Analogy: always a like comparison of two different things, i.e., "The wings of an airplane are like the wings of a bird."

Antagonist: villain.

Antonym: word meaning opposite of another, i.e., child/adult.

Bibliography: a list of books used as a reference found at the end of a report.

Character: an "actor" of the story.

Characterization: a portrayal of the subject by his/her mannerisms, speech, clothing, locale.

Cliché: overused, trite words or phrases, i.e., green-eyed monster (jealousy).

Composition: defining what type of writing, for example:
1. Prose: non-rhyming, ordinary language.
2. Poetry: specific formatted use of language, rhyming, sometimes not, using imagery and symbols.
3. Exposition: specific thematic writing; for example, term papers, reports.

Conflict: the problem between the protagonist (hero) and the antagonist (villain), stated in simple terms as: one against oneself; one against another; one against God.

Conflict/Resolution: characters change by solving problem(s).

Endnotes: formatted like footnotes, quotes and references in the text that are numbered but are listed at the end of the document. See examples of endnotes and footnotes on pages 31-32.

Figure of speech: words and phrases that create images. The most common figures of speech are:
1. Metaphor: likening images, i.e., comparing something to another thing, "My love is a red rose."
2. Simile: something similar to another using "like" or "as," "My love is like a red rose."

First draft: the working paper, including notes and ideas, but not the perfect, completed form.

Five senses of writing:
1. Voice: the overall "tone" of the writing, usually described as either active or passive: active verbs=active voice; passive verbs=passive voice, i.e., "books fell from the shelf"/ "books were falling from the shelf."
2. Impression: the appearance of the finished paper and overall feeling the reader is left with after having read the paper.
3. Grammatical sense: organization and rules of language, i.e., the elements of good writing.
4. Style: the "self" revealed in one's writing by use of language, like how the "self" is evident in one's walk, speech, and mannerisms.
5. Point of view (*POV*): train of thought of the one who is telling the story (the narrator) expressed as: emotions/opinions/references. Expressed reactions are based on what seems probable or true, but not concrete fact, or from a source of information deemed authoritative. All these fall under "point of view."

Footer: text at the bottom of the page (like the page number).

Footnotes: in the body of the text, a direct quote from a source with notations at the bottom of the page showing references. Ibid.: Latin term meaning "in the same place," to be used if the next numbered quote is from the same source; op.cit.: Latin term meaning "in the work previously quoted," referring back to a reference used in an earlier footnote.

Format: how the material is organized and arranged for a specific type of paper.

Genres: categories of books, i.e., fiction: mysteries, westerns, romance, mainstream, sci-fi, classic literature, children's literature, comic books, short stories; and non-fiction: reference, sports, biographies, cookbooks, self-help.

Header: line at the top of the page, usually with name/page number.

Identity: the personality of the characters.

Images/imagery: likeness to a person or object, used to evoke an idea of a person or object; imagery is metaphors, similes, allusions, figures of speech, paintings.

Lead sentence: opening "hook." Also, see *topic sentence.*

Literary elements, three basic: plot, character, and setting.

Media: radio, TV, newspapers, magazines, periodicals. (The singular of media is "medium.")

Myth/legend: story about people or events, real or fictional, that is handed down and accepted with a certain amount of truth.

Paper types: term paper, short story, essay, report, letter, journal and diaries.
1. Term paper: a paper that is researched, with noted references.
2. Short story: fiction, made-up events and characters.
3. Essay: writing on a particular subject, usually written as an opinion, as opposed to a term paper.
4. Report: an account of an event, as of a reading of a book.

5. Letter: a business or personal paper in a specific format.
6. Journal: a dated record of real events as they happened.
7. Diary: a personal account of events.

Parallel construction: the idea, subject and verb(s) agree; example: "Mary had a little lamb, as well as a ram, an ewe and a whole flock of sheep."

Passive/active voice: telling/showing.

Plagiarize: to rip off someone's idea and not give the author due credit.

Plot: storyline, the reasons why characters do what they do.

Protagonist: hero or heroine.

Redundancy: saying the same thing over and over and over again.

Sentence fragment (incomplete sentence): incomplete thought and an unforgivable sin in writing except for dialogue; a sentence without a subject and predicate, i.e., "The cat (*subject*) with one eye (*no predicate*)."

Setting: where the action takes place.

Symbols: something that represents an idea, figure, character, i.e., letters, numerals, peace sign.

Synonym: word meaning the same as another word example, i.e., child/kid.

Style: the "fashion" of writing; the way words "sound" on paper and reveal the self.

SASE: self-addressed, stamped envelope to be included with a letter asking for information.

Tense: "time" of the story (present, past or future); also, applies to verbs, as in 'tense agreement,' i.e., she was, they were, I am, he is, we are.

Tension: the "what's happening" that moves the story and keeps the reader interested in the characters.

Theme: topic/subject.

Topic sentence: the main idea of the paper found in the first paragraph.

Unity: what holds the idea of a paper together so the paper as a whole *flows* from the topic, from sentence to sentence, paragraph to paragraph, page to page.

Verbs: words of action or being. Effective writing uses active verbs (I move, I moved) rather than passive verbs (I was moving, I might move).

About the Author

Jacquie Ream was born June 10, 1952 in Oklahoma City, Oklahoma, and was raised in San Bernardino, California. She currently lives in Seattle, Washington, with her husband. Her daughter, Brandy, is serving in the United States Air Force.

She attended college on writing scholarships (Pitzer, Claremont and Cal-State SB) and completed her Master's degree in creative writing at the University of Washington.

"I benefited greatly from professional writing groups, and I have taught creative writing for ages five through sixty-five years old. I have written two adult novels, three children's books and numerous short stories. I should like my epitaph to read: 'She lived, she loved, she wrote.'"